Qi Gong & Form Introd

Contents

Introduction	5
Notes On Breathing	8
Dantien	11
Meridian Tapping	12
Qi Gong	14
10 Postures	16
13 Postures	29
18 Postures	63
The Tai Chi Form	111
What are the 13 Postures? (5 Steps, 8 Gates)	116
On Learning The Form	119
Review Of The Ten Essential Principles	122
Stances	124
Hand Shape	131
Direction: Your Back is to the North	132
Session Structure	135
Review of Movement Names 1st Section	137
Recommended Reading & Resources	138

Dedication
To Karen,
Joe & Ben.

Qi Gong & Form Introduction

Introduction to The Tai Chi Club

The challenge of Tai Chi Chuan is to Master yourself.

The vast majority of people new to Tai Chi Chuan will attend a Tai Chi session because the class is near to them. What will swing things as to whether you actually learn anything is if you practise, if you enjoy it and if you can understand the teacher. Once you have been practising for a while you will be in a stronger position to try other styles and teachers and attend courses.

Tai Chi Chuan & The Tai Chi Club
We practise Yang Style and the specific version we initially follow is Master Yang Jun Family Traditional Hand Form (103). You practise one move at a time, starting with the First Section which takes five minutes to perform slowly. If you did it quickly it would take under a minute. Because everything is new, once you've got the First Section under your belt, the rest is easier to learn because most of the stances are repeats and the ideas are similar. We practise by demonstration, body alignment (for example move your hands down towards the level of your waist) and meaning (how the move relates to the 13 postures or would be used if practising with a real person). The key to practising the Form is to grasp the idea that it is basically five ways of moving or standing and eight ways or strategies of dealing with

energy coming towards you from any direction. These are called the 13 postures.

Club Qi Gong
We practise various sets of Qi Gong (pronounced "Chee" as in "Cheese"). These exercises help you to relax and control your breathing and also to develop your sense of internal energy. The breathing methods are varied, the type we practise leads on to The Form and we try to practise in a straightforward manner. If you read about Qi Gong it all sounds very complicated. There are many works published on Qi Gong and Tai Chi Chuan of all styles and the authors of these founding books have spent a lifetime studying all aspects of the theory and background of the subject. Later books often just parrot earlier versions. Either way, it doesn't mean it's all true and you need to know everything. A cynic could comment the reason it all seems so complicated is because people feel they have to fill a book to sell it, rather than needing all the space in a book to describe the methods.

Irrespective, first you have to learn something from which to approach the subject and then you can seek out the information based on the style you are pursuing once you figure out which style that is. It's worth bearing in mind you can read as much as you like, but unless you want to practise, you won't end up with much to show for it other than companionship. If you miss this first step, the rest will remain a mystery.

This book concentrates in the main on the '*Doing*' side of Tai Chi Chuan and as a reference for those people attending sessions. Tai Chi Chuan and Qi Gong can help bring you health and contentment because you try to take on this mind set.

You can look to the past and decide everything was better. You can look to the future and hope everything will get better. You can live in the present and decide to be better.

That choice to decide to enjoy life is one you make, it can't be made for you. The choice to learn Qi Gong or Tai Chi Chuan is one you must make happen by setting your mind and practising, it can't be learnt for you. The first time you practise you are as good as you can be, so enjoy being that and go easy on yourself rather than concerned about being better than anyone else. After a few weeks you may think, "I'm better now". After a few years you may think, "I'm better now". But how you feel in the moment is where the enjoyment is to be found.

Notes on Breathing

Breathing should be natural, not forced. Breathe out first to set a level playing field. When you feel the need to take a breath, begin. Breathe 'In' to the count of four and 'Out' to a count of five, then continue to slow down your breathing further as you progress.

1. Breathe through your nose. The mouth is lightly closed but not sealed tightly and the tongue gently touches the roof of the mouth just above the two front teeth (some curl the tip of the tongue). The emphasis is on naturalness and spontaneity. As you practise a natural rhythm will result without any conscious effort. This method is how we breathe doing the Tai Chi Chuan Form and helps you to avoid getting dry within the mouth and build up saliva which is swallowed.

2. Breathe in through your nose and out through your mouth. This method is more common to many Qi Qong exercises and Hard style martial arts as it allows you to expel the breath powerfully and with raised spirits. It may lead you to becoming dry if you practise over long periods of time (See "Heng Ha" breathing on p10).

This is all you will really tend to end up doing irrespective of what you study. However, people like to know more so here's some additional information:

Additional Breathing Methods
The first point to remember is you are going to breathe so don't get wound up about it. Apart from the above advice, you are far better reading up. It gets really confusing when you talk to people on the spot. Some like to feel they are doing something different while they do the various routines and practise various breathing techniques. You don't have to do everything the same way every time. For example, instead of practising the precise movements of the Form your concentration is placed into trying out a breathing pattern.

Natural Breath.
In general, you breathe 'Out' on extending your movements and 'In' on closing, but there are exceptions such as in the 13 Postures Qi Gong breathing set. For example, when pushing out you tend to be on the

'Out' breath, when drawing yourself in you tend to be on the 'In' breath. You will find you are already doing this. Try lifting a full kettle and thinking about your breathing. You'll find you take a breath and lift because you are lifting up, not pushing out. Now try lifting the heavy kettle while breathing out. It will feel more uncomfortable. Like weight lifting where you breathe 'In' to pull up and 'Out' to expand this type of breathing is often referred to as 'After Heaven Breathing'. The type of breath you take after birth and are already doing.

Before Heaven Breathing
Same as above 'timing wise' during the Form. Pre-birth breathing imitates the supposed general breathing of a baby in the womb. Through the umbilical cord the baby receives oxygen and nutrition and eliminates through the same path. This ends when the cord is cut. It's generally described as a person who contracts the abdomen upon inhalation and expands during expiration. Often known as 'Reverse Breathing'. As you breathe 'In' your stomach looks like it goes in and as you breathe 'Out' it looks like it goes out.

During static Qi Gong exercises imagine breath travelling up your back on the 'In' and down the front on the 'Out' in a circular motion. There are other methods but after a while, you tend to stick to one and generally give it no thought. It should not be made into a big deal. As my wife points out, if I could learn to breathe through my ears I might be onto something.

Small Circulation Breathing
Imagination. Inhale and exhale through the nose. Breath travels up the back and down the front to Dantien (Imagined centre point of your body if you were dangling from a string running down through your head / torso). Done as Natural or Reverse breathing.

Cleansing Breath
Kind of deep breath you take in open spaces, by the sea. 'In' through the nose 'Out' through the mouth. Emphasizes exhalation, which is longer than inhaling.

Tonic Breath
Other way around. Inhaling 'In' through the mouth and 'Out' through the nose. Kind of breath one takes before diving.

Long Breath / Abdominal post-birth breath
When inhaling the lower abdomen expands because of the air coming in and contracts as the air comes out. You would appear not to be expanding your chest, you are pushing or pulling the breath down further to the Dantien (in your imagination).

Alternate Breath
Inhaling through one nostril and exhaling out the other. Said to help relieve headaches and stress. If the pain is on the right side of the head, inhale through the right nostril, if it's on the left, inhale through the left. If it's on both sides of your head, go home and lie down.

Tortoise or Slow Breath
Being able to comfortably slow your breath down to 3 - 4 breaths per minute.

"Heng Ha"
The noise Yang Lu Chan was said to have heard while watching the Chen family train in secret. It would seem this requires breathing / exhaling in part through the mouth as you can't make any sound if you don't. First practise breathing naturally in the Pre-Birth method. When "Heng" is sounded, pull in the breath, when "Ha" is sounded push it out.

In Through The Nose / Out Through The Mouth With Spirit
Very popular martial arts breathing style. "Ha!" or "Kia!". The sound is a raw explosion of energy and breath. It serves to raise the spirits, increase power and time the breath to the strike. It also means you hopefully don't get hit while breathing in (which winds you). In Ju-Jitsu and Judo you are encouraged to breathe out on a fall to avoid injury, if you breathe in while falling that tends to hurt more. This is perhaps why people instinctively scream as they hurtle off the top of a building, but that won't work.

There are more ways to perform breathing exercises. What weight you lend to it is a personal experience. Either way, once you breathe out, breathe in. Focus on your middle body point (Dantien) when performing the exercises. This is just below your navel in the imagined mid centre point of your body.

Dantien (Dan t'ian, dan tien or tan t'ien)

Dan = Essence or Energy, *Tien* = Field or Area. A vast topic intrinsic to Chinese medicine and the location where it is believed the Qi or vital energy is stored and distributed throughout the body. There are said to be three Dantiens in the body. The upper in the brain just behind a point directly between the eyebrows and corresponding to the Third Eye. The middle in the heart and the lower described as being located 1.3 inches below the navel in the imagined centre point of your body.
The general philosophical idea is using your imagination you drive energy to the Lower Dantien (towards the abdomen). This area then stores your Qi or vital energy which you can then accumulate over a period of time by performing passive Qi Gong exercises.

Balance Point
From a practical point of view the Lower Dantien is the centre point of gravity within the middle of your body. Being aware and controlling your own centre of balance while finding and controlling it in others is a fundamental to practising Tai Chi Chuan.

Meridian Tapping

This is done as a warm up exercise and also helps raise your spirits. The tingling you feel in your hands after completing the set is a similar feeling to the early sensations of Qi or the feeling of your own body energy. The idea is that if you can recognise this sensation, you go on to feel it in other areas of Tai Chi and Qi Gong without the tapping.

Start in Preparation Form position (Stand naturally)
Warm your hands by rubbing together then tap with both hands the following:

> Top of both feet
> Up outside of both legs
> Down inside of both legs
> Hips and Dantien
> Up front of body, and across chest
> Back of left hand, up arm to shoulder
> Turn arm over, down left arm to palm
> Back of right hand, up arm to shoulder
> Turn arm over, down right arm to palm
> Tap nape of neck, up and over back of head
> Either side of forehead

Massage Head/Face
Rub the nape of the neck with both hands. Then use two fingers to massage the ear lobes, across the forehead, the top of eyebrows and either side of nose and under the cheekbones. Resume tapping down and up the left arm, repeat with the right arm back down finishing at the palms. This type of massage can be very effective if done to areas of tension. You can use the front or back of your fingers and hands. If you use this technique on other people around the shoulder and neck areas it can quickly relieve stress and tense muscles. The areas will warm up on their own when being tapped, but using good quality Tiger Balm (don't buy cheap) will help enhance the sensation of warmth and relief. If after performing the tapping for ten minutes you pull your palms away gently and hold them close to the shoulder area you may find the other person is still aware of the place your hand is hovering above and feel a sense of continued energy and warmth with or without the balm.

Don't read into this more than there is. Some refer to this as healing, but some people get carried away. It is however a pleasurable experience.

Meridian Theory

The idea is Meridians link the top of the body to the bottom, one side to the other and inside to out. Blockages cause problems, so you try to keep each pathway free and open. All these exercises are perhaps best thought of as preventive, like good diet, or to help recover from a medical event or illness. To put it in perspective, if you did find yourself involved in a serious accident, are you going to call for a Doctor or a Masseur? On the other hand, if you can treat yourself for stress and minor pains, what have you got to lose? One does not rule out the other.

Qi Gong

The definition of Qi Gong is Qi means energies and Gong (from gongfu) means any training taking a long time and effort to learn the subject.

The *Tai Chi Club* perform three sets of Qi Gong to lead on to the Tai Chi Chuan Form and as a relaxation technique.

1. Breathe out so you feel there is the requirement to take a deep breath.
2. Breathe through your nose throughout the exercise with your mouth lightly towards closed but not tense or tightly shut. Your tongue touches the roof of your mouth just above the two front teeth. You can allow breath through your mouth if you feel happier.
3. Breathe deeply down to your abdomen (Dantien) but not forced.
4. Initially, count while you breathe, one count longer out than in.
5. Slow your breathing down. Add a number or two to the count.

This breathing method can also be practised to help deal with anxiety and panic attacks. These breathing control techniques may not be suitable if you have a chronic lung condition. Stand naturally with your knees neither locked nor bent. When you breathe out, think in terms of letting go of tension. It is better to do just one exercise a day for a minute or two at a regular time (while you make a cup of tea in the morning for example) than practise erratically.

Explanation
1. Breathing out first is to set the field to gain control.
2. Helps deal with hyperventilating, panic attacks and also helps towards building up saliva in your mouth which stops you getting dry.
3. Helps stretch the diaphragm and relax the stomach muscles when it becomes hard to breathe.
4. Counting helps combat against panicky breathing and slows down the breathing process.
5. Breathing out one beat longer helps empty the lungs to take in more air.

Once you've finished a routine walk around a little before beginning another. The eventual aim is to bring into harmony your Essence,

Energy and Spirit.
If you imagine your Energy (breath) going up and down your body, your blood and Spirit follows helping build up and strengthen your Essence. Each one needs and helps the other.

In basic approach, think of it this way. You get delivery of a new train containing original sealed oils (Original Source) and a core fuel supply. It also must convert oxygen and water. The train is born. You buy in more fuel to run the train but it's not quite the same as the original supply and cannot replace the original oils (at this external level) which have to be guarded. This new fuel contains its' own Essence which adds a little to your supply (and the well-being of the entire train). It also contains energy of which the majority will be used to power every aspect of the train. The train still goes nowhere until you add a driver. The driver represents the Spirit of the train. It tries to control how much Energy (from the fuel) to use but also tries to keep a little to add to the back up supply (as Essence) but struggles to touch the original oils. All three work together helping each other. The train (Essence), the fuel (a bit of Essence, but mainly Energy) and the driver (Spirit), otherwise you just end up with a stationary train, a pile of coke and a driver walking home.
In the real world, it is going to add up to you standing or sitting in a place breathing deeply. If you feel you enjoy the experience of that, then our Qi Gong exercises can be done as a form of health, deep exercise and meditation.

Relax
In the beginning, relax into the 'Out' breath. So as you breathe in imagine the energy travelling up your body and as you breathe out, imagine it travelling down to the soles of your feet. Try not to hold your weight in your knees. And by 'Relax' we don't mean limp, but rather open and extended. You stretch, but not to the point of over extension. You should feel energised inside and in control.

Illness
Many people are drawn to these exercises because they have suffered an illness or devastating loss of health and mobility. Trying to learn before you get ill is very good advice because all exercise is good advice if done sensibly.

10 Postures

If you want to concentrate on breathing methods this Qi Gong is ideal because the movements are relatively easy to learn.

Stand relaxed, hands one on top of other, palms up.

(Male right hand on top / female left)
Breathe in / out through the nose.

You breathe in and out on each posture.

1. Open palm up, as demonstrated. Breathe in and out.
2. Turn forearms / palms over. Breathe in and out.
3. Raise up to chest height. Turn forearms / palms face up. Breathe in and out.
4. Turn forearms / palms face down. Breathe in and out.
5. Raise up to look through palms eye level. Breathe in and out.
6. Open arms / palms facing each other shoulder width. Breathe in and out.
7. Push out palms facing out. Breathe in and out.
8. Sink down. Palm / arms facing floor. Breathe in and out.
9. Turn in. Breathe in and out.
10 Turn forearms / palms up. Breathe in and out.
Close.

Qi Gong & Form Introduction

Qi Gong
10 Postures

Stand relaxed, with your hands one on top of other, palms up.

(Male right hand on top / female left)

Breathe out.

Move 1

Open your palm facing up. Breathe in and out. Count to four in and count to five out. The idea is to slow your breathing down.

Breathing out first sets a good level and encourages you to take a long breath in.

Move 2

Turn forearms / palms over.

Breathe in and out. Count to four in and count to five out.

Move 3

Raise up to chest height.
Turn forearms / palms face up.
Breathe in and out.

Move 4

Turn forearms / palms face down.
Breathe in and out.

Move 5

Raise up to look through palms eye level.
Breathe in and out.

Move 6

Open arms / palms facing each other shoulder width.
Breathe in and out.

Move 7

Push out, palms facing out.
Breathe in and out.

Move 8

Sink down. Palms / arms facing floor.
Breathe in and out.

Move 9

Turn in.
Breathe in and out.

Qi Gong & Form Introduction

Move 10

Turn forearms / palms up.
Breathe in and out.

Close

Bring palms in together towards your middle body (Dantien).

Close.

13 Postures

This is not the same as the 5 steps, 8 Energies (13 Postures) of Tai Chi Chuan.

This Qi Gong is done in a more flowing manner than 10 Postures. The postures and breathing should be natural and not as fixed as the drawings imply. The breathing and count is inserted as a guide. There are places where extra opening and closing breaths could be inserted depending on the practise speed.

There are also different ways of counting the moves. 1, 2, 12 & 13 are repeats.

Moves 6, 7, 8, 9, 10 & 11 combine one breath in and one breath out.

Once you have practised for a while, aim to be natural and make it your own.

Stand relaxed, hands one on top of other, palms up. (Male right hand on top / female left) Parallel Stance. Breathe out.
1. Open palms out to side, shoulder width, towards upwards as demonstrated. Breathe in to open, then out to close.
2. Open palms out to side wider than shoulder width, towards upwards. Breathe in to open, then out to close.
3. Open palms out to side wider than shoulder width, towards upwards. Breathe in to open. Bring in both hands, bend down sinking towards floor. Right hand leads. Draw a circle (left C/W. Right A/C) with both

hands, breathing out.

4. Go back to vertical. Breathing in. Turn palms up, push out towards front, breathe out.

5. Turn palms outwards. Swim out. Breathe in. Turn palms in. Bring arms in. Breathe out.

6. Turn palms down, push down. Breathe in.

7. Circle arms open, palms still facing down. Breathe out.

8. Rotate palms face up. Circle upwards. Arms above head to centre. Breathe in.

9. Start to breathe out. Point fingers towards ground, Backs of hands facing each other.

10. Turn palms over at bottom of previous move. Scoop upwards along centre line above head. Breathe in.

11. Turn forearms outwards. Draw large circle from top to bottom. Palms coming towards each other. Breathe out.

12. Open palms out to side wider than shoulder width, towards upwards. Breathe in to open then out to close.

13. Open palms out to side, shoulder width, towards upwards as demonstrated. Breathe in to open then out to close.

13 Postures
Done to 10 breaths

Stand relaxed, with your hands one on top of other, palms up.

(Male right hand on top / female left)

Breathe out.

Move 1

Open palms out to side, shoulder width, towards upwards as demonstrated. Breathe in to open.

Move 1a

Bring arms in, palms towards upwards. Breathe out.

Move 2

Open palms out to side slightly wider than Move 1, shoulder width, towards upwards as demonstrated. Breathe in to open.

Move 2a

Bring arms in, palms towards upwards. Breathe out.

Move 3

Open palms out to side, shoulder width, towards upwards as demonstrated. Breathe in to open.

Move 3a

Bring arms in as demonstrated.
Begin to breathe out.

Move 3b

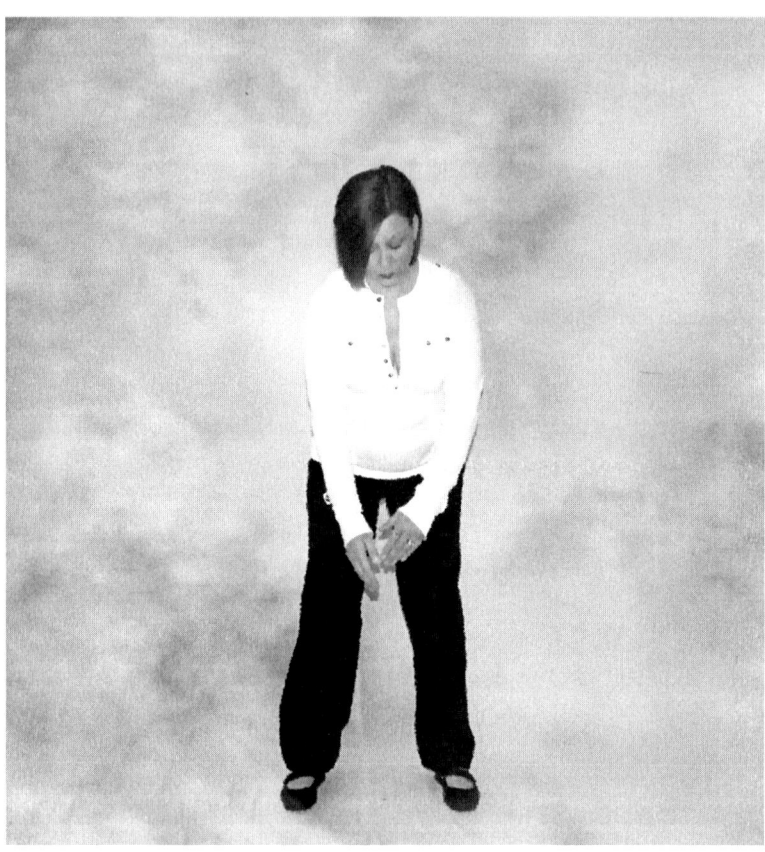

Continue to breathe out. Start to bend forward bringing palms towards each other in a downwards direction allowing your knees to relax into the movement following your toes direction.

Move 3c

Begin to breathe in. Circle arms & hands left anti-clockwise, right clockwise. Begin to rise, palms slightly facing up.

Move 4

Continue to rise, breathing in.

Move 4a

Turn palms outwards, pushing forward at chest height. Begin to breathe out.

Move 4b

Continue to extend your arms and push forwards.
Breathe out.

Move 5

Begin to breathe in.
Open arms towards the sides.

Move 5a

Continue to breathe in. Extend arms out to sides, palms down.

Move 5b

Begin to breathe out. Rotate arms, palms facing up.

Move 6

Bring arms to front, rotating elbows, palms facing out.
Breathing out.

Move 6a

Breathe in. Lower arms pushing down, palms facing down.

Move 7

Circle arms open, palms still facing down. Breathing out.

Move 8

Open arms out to side rotating palms up.
Beginning to breathe in.

Move 8a

Continue to the top, breathing in. Rotate arms up drawing a circle, palms facing up.

Move 9

Start to breathe out. Point fingers towards ground,
Backs of hands facing each other.

Move 9a

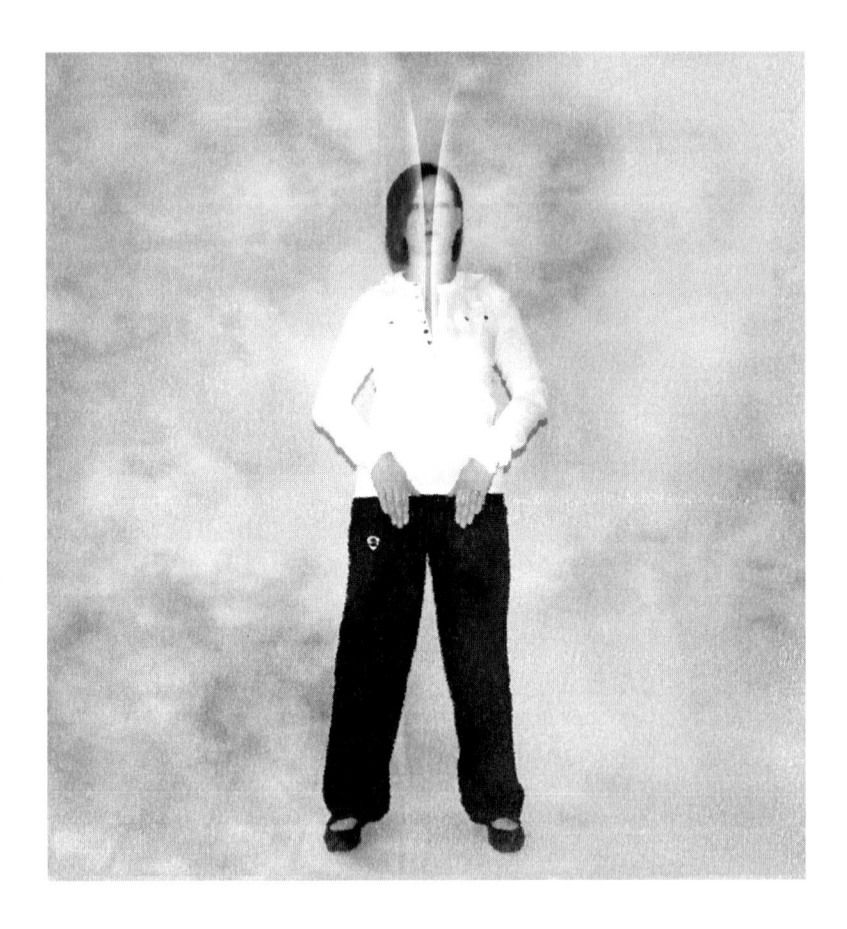

Breathe out. Dropping arms following your centre line and sinking.

Qi Gong & Form Introduction

Move 10

Begin to breathe in. Sink palms then turning to face up.

Move 10a

Lift palms following your centre line. Breathe in.

Move 11

Turn forearms outwards. Start to breathe out.

Move 11a

Continue to breathe out. Allowing arms to sink drawing a circle.

Move 11b

Breathe out. Completing the circle with palms facing up.

Move 12

Open palms out to side slightly wider than shoulder width. Breathe in to open.

Move 12a

Bring arms in, palms towards upwards. Breathe out.

Move 13

Open palms out to side, shoulder width, slightly less wide. Breathe in to open.

Move 13a

Bring arms in, palms towards upwards. Start to breathe out.

Close

Bring palms in together towards your middle body (Dantien).

Close.

18 Postures

Stand relaxed, hands one on top of other, palms up. (Male right hand on top / female left) Parallel Stance. Breathe out.

1. Open arms out to side beginning the in breath. Raising up, shoulder height, palms downwards, sink elbows, continue to breathe in. Push out to sides as demonstrated, beginning the out breath and continue to breathe out.
2. Bring left arm towards right, palms down, crossing wrists, left under right, breathing in. Begin breathing out, turn left arm. Rotating waist. Then wrists towards upwards. Allowing both arms to sink down towards sides, breathing out.
3. Open arms out to side and raising up, shoulder height, palms downwards, sink elbows, breathing in. Push out to sides as demonstrated, breathing out.
4. Bring arms in towards centre making fists. Breathe in.
5. Turn fists outwards, opening into Tiger Mouth. Extending arms out to side, breathe out.
6. Bring arms in towards centre. Begin breathing in. Make fists. Breathe in.
7. Turn fists outwards. Extending up arms. Cross wrists, breathing out.
8. Draw a circle with both arms moving sideways and downward. Continue the circle to halfway breathing in. Begin breathing out halfway down. Continue to breathe out to finish the circle. Palms end facing up breathing out.
9. Turn head sideways to left, breathing in. Turn to face front to breathe out.
10. Turn head sideways to right, breathing in. Turn to face front to breathe out.

11. Curve arms up towards chest starting to breathe in. Turn arms so palms face towards down. Track down legs bending over starting to breath out and scoop water breathing out.
12. Stand up, lift up arms to centre starting to breathe in.
13. Turn to left and extend left arm towards sky and right arm pushing and extending out towards ground. Breathe out.
14. Level off breathing in.
15. Turn to right and extend right arm towards sky and left arm pushing and extending out towards ground. Breathe out.
16. Level off and sink elbows. Breathing in. Push out arms breathing out.
17. Bring left arm towards right, palms down, crossing wrists, left under right, breathing in. Starting to breathe out, turn left, then right wrist towards upwards. Allowing both arms to sink down towards centre, beginning to breathe out. Breathe out as both arms sink.
18. Open arms to side, breathe in. Close arms to centre. Breathe out. Bring palms in together towards your middle body (Dantien).
Close.

Qi Gong & Form Introduction

18 Postures
Done to 14 breaths

Stand relaxed, with your hands one on top of other, palms up.

(Male right hand on top / female left)

Breathe out.

Qi Gong & Form Introduction

Move 1

Open arms out to side beginning the in breath.

Move 1a

Raising up, shoulder height, palms downwards, sink elbows, continue to breathe in.

Move 1b

Push out to sides as demonstrated, beginning the out breath and continue to breathe out.

Move 2

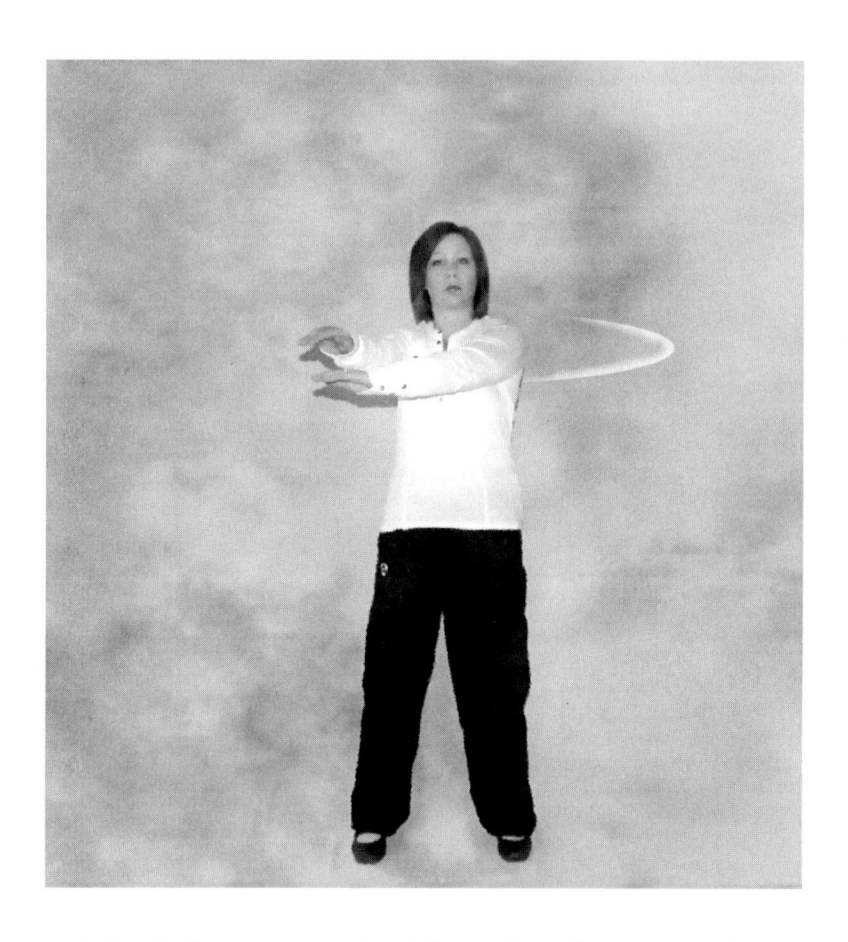

Bring left arm towards right, palms down, crossing wrists, left under right, breathing in.

Move 2a

Begin breathing out, turn left arm.

Move 2b

Rotating waist.

Move 2c

Then wrists towards upwards.

Move 2d

Allowing both arms to sink down towards sides, breathing out.

Qi Gong & Form Introduction

Move 3

Open arms out to side and raising up, shoulder height, palms downwards, sink elbows, breathing in.

Move 3a

Raising up, shoulder height, palms downwards, sink elbows, breathe in.

Move 3b

Push out to sides as demonstrated, to breathe out.

Move 4

Bring arms in towards centre making fists.
Breathe in.

Move 5

Turn fists outwards, opening into Tiger Mouth.
Begin the out breath.

Move 5a

Extending arms out to side, breathe out.

Move 6

Bring arms in towards centre. Begin breathing in.

Qi Gong & Form Introduction

Move 6a

Make fists. Breathe in.

Move 7

Begin breathing out. Turn fists outwards. Extending up arms.

Qi Gong & Form Introduction

Move 7a

Cross wrists, breathing out.

Move 8

Draw a circle with both arms moving sideways and downward beginning to breathe in.

Qi Gong & Form Introduction

Move 8a

Continue the circle to breathing in to halfway.

Qi Gong & Form Introduction

Move 8b

Begin breathing out.

Move 8c

Continue to breathe out to finish the circle.

Move 8d

Palms end facing up, breathing out.

Move 9

Turn head sideways to left, breathing in.

Qi Gong & Form Introduction

Move 9a

Turn to face front to breathe out.

Move 10

Turn head sideways to right, breathing in.

Move 10a

Turn to face front to breathe out.

Qi Gong & Form Introduction

Move 11

Curve arms up towards chest starting to breathe in.

Move 11a

Turn arms so palms face towards down.
Breathe in.

Qi Gong & Form Introduction

Move 11b

Track down legs bending over starting to breathe out.

Move 11c

Scoop water. Breathing out.

Move 12

Stand up, lift up arms to centre starting to breathe in.

Move 13

Turn to left and extend left arm towards sky and right arm pushing and extending out towards ground. Breathe out.

Qi Gong & Form Introduction

Move 14

Level off, breathing in.

Move 15

Turn to right and extend right arm towards sky and left arm pushing and extending out towards ground. Breathe out.

Move 16

Level off and sink elbows. Breathing in.

Move 16a

Push out arms breathing out.

Move 17

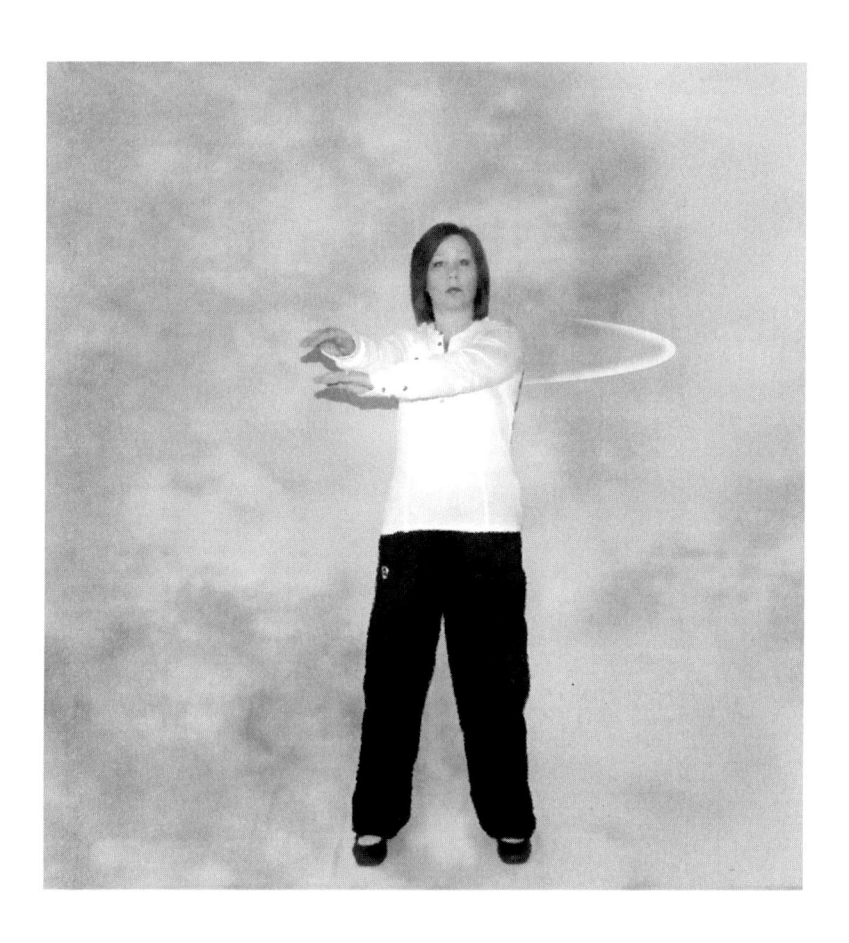

Bring left arm towards right, palms down, crossing wrists, left under right, breathing in.

Qi Gong & Form Introduction

Move 17a

Starting to breathe out, turn using waist movement towards the left.

Move 17b

Then right wrist towards upwards, turn towards the front.

Move 17c

Allowing both arms to sink down towards centre, beginning to breathe out.

Qi Gong & Form Introduction

Move 17d

Breathe out as both arms sink.

Move 18

Open arms to side, breathe in.

Move 18a

Close arms to centre. Breathe out.

Close

Bring palms in together towards your middle body (Dantien).

Close.

The Tai Chi Form

A brief introduction to where the Form came from and what it is.

Yang Tai Chi Chuan was created by Yang Lu Chan. The name is spelt differently depending on which source you refer to.

Why Are There So Many Yang Styles?
Pre Yang Lu Chan, there was no Yang style. Everybody claiming to practise Yang Style Tai Chi will say they can trace their teachings back to the founder of the style, Yang Lu Chan. Nobody disputes Yang Lu Chan created it. Prior to Yang Style there was Chen style and prior to that there were forms (Monastery Styles) created which are acknowledged as Tai Chi Chuan by historical figures such as Chang San Feng over 700 years ago. Chang San Feng had learnt Shaolin Temple Boxing (Kung Fu), which was introduced by the Buddhist and First Patriarch of China, Bodhidharma in the sixth Century. He had travelled to Shaolin from India, having himself been taught by an Indian guy within the Royal court of his father who was a King. Of course he was, but nobody gives the Indian guy much credit. Just kidding, he's a very famous Zen Master*. Apparently, the Chang San Feng version is disputed, historians have suggested the legend stems from a 17th century Qi Gong manual known as the Yijin Jing. Isn't Google wonderful?

Yang Lu Chan. Old Frame. (1799-1872).
1 man. 1 style.

Yang Lu Chan originally received instruction from his peers including Cheng De Hu & Chen Chang Xing (Chen Style). He then took this background and became known as the founder of Yang Style Tai Chi Chuan. In later life Yang Lu Chan created a name for himself as a fighter of extraordinary ability and was called upon to teach the Royal Court.
He was said to have taught them a diluted style (Park Style), only teaching the full versions and ideas in secret to close male family. In the fullness of time, both were then taught to other people. It was carried on in the family name by his children (not without complaint or dispute).

*Prajnatara - 27th Indian Osho Zen Master

Yang Lu Chan also taught non family members who spent their lives learning and also achieved very high status and respect as carriers of the Yang style. There is still the idea put forward that all the secrets are only revealed to close family members and students, but since you can't prove a negative, it remains a rumour. Most of the ideas have been used by other styles and martial arts and it's a fair assumption that the supposed secret information is readily accessible anyway.

T. T. Liang was said to have remarked Ch'eng Man-ch'ing waited years to reveal to him the secrets of Tai Chi Fa Jing breathing which was "Breathe out on the release of energy." This is beginners instruction in Karate and hard style arts.*

So we have Yang Lu Chan + Disciples + two surviving children, Yang Ban Hou (did a version called Small Frame) & Yang Jian Hou (Medium Frame). These people also taught non family members who spent their lives learning the style and teaching. You get the plot. Everyone went on to teach everyone else, all claiming a direct link to the founder, Yang Lu Chan. From generation to generation, plus all the associated teachers, Disciples and off-shoot Yang styles. In addition the idea of Yang Tai Chi for health also materialised distancing itself from the idea of Tai Chi Chuan as a fighting art.

It's only recently that film of any Yang style has been widely available to even begin to be able to judge how styles within Yang differ. Prior to that, like Chinese whispers there was probably never a definitive presentation as the aim was to be a superior fighter, not achieve a high level of pedantry.

Yang Cheng Fu. *Grandson of Yang Lu Chan and son of Jian Hou (1883-1936).*

Yang Cheng Fu is important because he wrote his version of the Form down calling it Large Frame (including photographs) setting it in stone so to speak and it was translated in the West to English. Be clear, Yang Cheng Fu did not publish Lu Chans' (Old), Ban Hous' (Small) or Jian Hous' (Medium) frame Tai Chi Chuan Form, so anybody following Cheng Fu is not doing the exact version of Lu Chan including Cheng Fu.
But Yang Cheng Fu had received instruction from his surviving family

Page 26-27. Tai Chi The Supreme Ultimate. Lawrence Galante. ISBN 0-87728-497-0

members and peers and was also acknowledged as an extraordinary fighter. He was a widespread teacher, and he made the Form standardised and more accessible. He also taught Cheng Man-ch'ing who went on to popularise Yang Style Tai Chi Chuan in America in the second part of the 20th Century. Though this was not the Yang long form. This is still a very sore point with many. It also important again to stress Cheng Man-ch'ing learnt the long form first including the martial applications as well as creating his own short form.

There is no film footage of Yang Cheng Fu (as far as I know). Only the books. His nephew Fu Zhongwen (1903-1994) is arguably a person who closest resembles the form of Cheng Fu. There is film footage of him which you can pick up from You Tube. There is also film of Yang Shou Zhong (1911-1986) another son of Yang Cheng Fu. Again his form is unarguably a direct version of Yang Cheng Fu showing fast kicks.

About Health Forms
Health forms are generally based on Martial Tai Chi Chuan even if the instructor of the new style doesn't know it, or the meanings. A five year old can show you how the movement of a closed hand technique could be used as a punch. Many of the circular movements contained in Tai Chi health forms are also based on creating arm locks, throws, hitting pressure points and redirecting attacks.

All Tai Chi Chuan can be done as a Health Form and specifically Yang Cheng Fu devised his form as a Health Form version for the majority he demonstrated it to. It's important to remember Yang Cheng Fu also knew much of his family fighting forms, so when you read of his exploits, it doesn't follow because you have learnt his version of the Yang Family Form you have learnt what he was taught. His counterparts of the time also disagreed with the changes and methods and felt he was tampering with the Form by over simplifying the steps and stances, standardising the speed and removing some jumps and stamps. In other words, Yang Cheng Fu's version was intended to be more approachable to learn and teach in comparison to the methods of his forebearers. Many of the stances are simple and difficult turns and jumps are removed.

What are The Yang Traditional Hand Forms?
The Forms are a crib, a tick list, a reminder, a secret kept from the casual observer. A literal Chinese Whisper done physically. Once learnt it contains the ideas of Tai Chi Chuan as a martial art but like all martial arts the edge is lost if everybody can do it. In modern times the emphasis is on improving health and confidence by exercising both the body and mind. In that way it can be passed on from one person to another. How much of its' message is carried is completely dependent on how much you and your previous teachers know and how hard you study and seek out the knowledge. It suffers exactly the same problems as any Chinese Whisper in that each time it's taught to somebody else, parts are lost and parts are added because none of us are robots. It's also the reason the Form is kept concise by the various family members so as to preserve and teach it. Family members do it slightly differently depending on whom taught them and what interpretation they are placing on it. Also the moves can be counted differently. For instance Grasp the Birds' Tail consists of Ward Off Right, Ward Off Left, Roll Back, Press and Push. So is it one move, five or six? The five moves appear many times within other named sections as do portions of Grasp the Birds' Tail.

The modern focus in general is on preserving the appearance of the Form as a major goal.
Nobody does it the same way internally and an accurate representation of the form visually may be completely void of any meaning. In other words just a mime. A really difficult incredibly skilful mime, but still just a mime. What separates the two versions are trying to learn and to take on board the idea of the 13 postures, that each movement contains those ideas and then understanding the energies you are using and (in your imagination) trying to control from another person to make it work.

You don't have to practise on real people to imagine the way you might be pulling or pushing them and still gain great benefits from learning the Form. In fact it is incredibly important you pretend you are practising with a friend, relative or lover the ideas of the Form, otherwise you will not relax enough and start to feel aggressive. The idea is to avoid tension because that will slow you down and be draining on your spirits. You would however have to practise extremely hard with friends to learn to fight in a real situation. Push

Hands is a training method which can be great fun to have a go at. Like all martial arts, most of it wouldn't work because real people don't hit you how you want them to and vary in their own ability, size and age.

In other words any adult would stand a fair chance of defeating a child, but how many would defeat a heavy weight boxing champion? All fights are decided by the sex, age, size, level of ability and how many people are fighting. The more you practise, the more you gain an edge, but there is no certainty of winning no matter who you are. The quickest short cut to learning Tai Chi Chuan as a fighting art is to learn a Hard Style to the same degree, then you don't care if it works. So you can do Tai Chi for health and Tai Chi Chuan the martial art. The easiest way to learn both is trying to understand the 13 Postures of Tai Chi Chuan. What separates the two is how much you practise and with what intent.

What are the 13 Posture?

There are 5 Steps:
Forwards, Back, (Look) Left, (Gaze) Right, Centre.

There are 8 Gates or Energies:
Ward Off, Roll Back, Press, Push, Pull, Split, Elbow Strike, Shoulder Stroke.

In theory every movement within the Form has the potential to mix up the Steps and the Gates. When we do the Form we do Ward Off Left stepping *Forwards*, turning to the *Right*, looking to the *Right*, connect, *Pull* and *Split*, but you could do it with the same steps with a *Pull* and *Roll Back*, or *Pull* and *Shoulder Stroke*. But the second two would not look as much like the Form.

Think of it this way, when you move your hand away from your body in a palm shape forwards, in your imagination you could be *Pushing* your palm forwards or *Pulling* something with a thin wire under tension from behind, like on an exercise machine. While you know what energy you are applying, the move looks the same. However, because you are facing and looking forwards, people assume when they are learning that it's a push, but in your imagination you could be responding to an approach from any angle including from behind and be grabbing, *pulling* or leading away.

Read that last paragraph very carefully. It is the absolute key to why people misunderstand the ideas behind Tai Chi Chuan and constantly jump to conclusions.

On the five steps
Forwards, Back, (Look) Left, (Gaze) Right, Centre (Central equilibrium).

First of all the obvious, the idea is to teach you to move in any direction, and think in terms of moving up and down as well. You practise moving forwards, backwards, left or right or staying where you are and keeping your balance. However, each move in Tai Chi Chuan does not mean one thing, it is done in relation to what is happening around you. It means you can be doing any of the steps with central equilibrium. For example, while you might be physically moving forwards, if your imaginary opponent is behind you, you are moving away from them. If your opponent is standing to your left, you are moving sideways to their right while still physically moving forwards.

On the Eight Energies / Gates
You rarely just do one energy. So if you imagine pushing somebody, they must first be 'Up rooted'. This basically means off balance. Imagine you are a nine stone lady who is facing a twenty stone man. It would be very hard to push him over. Now imagine he was just starting to walk down a flight of stairs and you gave him a push from behind. As he plummeted down the steps he'd sound like an EastEnders theme tune. Now, imagine the twenty stone man moves forward to grab the nine stone lady around the shoulders and she lifts up both arms and grabs both his wrists pulling them forwards (I'm not saying it would be easy), but this is one example of the Wave or Beginning Posture done as a Double Ward Off and Pull.
Because he was already moving forwards and is now being pulled forwards, the feeling would be similar to falling down the stairs, at that point he may fall down, but the chances are he would instinctively correct his own momentum by stamping down his front foot and starting to correct his balance by pulling backwards. That's when you Push (and to be technical, with more energy in one of your arms and opposite back leg than the other to avoid being double weighted) without going beyond your balance point.
So your Push adds to his pulling away and hopefully he's now really off balance. He's already applying enough energy to correct his balance from your Pull by going backwards. The last thing he needs is you adding to his momentum with a Push. It is also the reason why you can only ever react to what another person is doing to perform Tai Chi Chaun. If the nine stone lady pushed back head on against the twenty stone man she would lose. If the twenty stone man pushed back head on against the nine stone lady he would still win. In that situation (if both do not have any fighting training) he has no need of Tai Chi Chuan, he would need it against someone of equal or bigger proportions than himself.
Put simply, you try to get a person off balance and add more energy where they were already moving bearing in mind they weren't planning on moving that way in the first place. Either a small or large person could however react to being pushed by stepping to the side

and pushing the other in the direction they were already travelling. It only works if the person is already moving or at least has the intent to move. You cannot effectively pull or push anybody using this idea if they are significantly bigger than you, are grounded or a dead weight. If you are doing Tai Chi for health it's irrelevant if it works anyway, that understanding tells you where to put your body and what energy you are trying to produce.

The theory is very simple, but in practice, it is not.

Understanding Energy
Trying to show somebody the Yang Hand Form without the idea of the 13 Postures or basic meanings of movements is like trying to show somebody how to serve a tennis ball without telling them you are playing tennis. They would copy the movement and wouldn't have a clue what energy to apply. So they would copy your mime. Now tell them they are serving a tennis ball in their imagination. You are holding a racket and throwing up a ball. So your right hand is not a fist at all and your left hand is cupped to release a ball. They would copy the move perfectly and understand completely how that would feel and what type of energy to use to get the ball to hit the racket three feet above their head. Now in their imagination they are playing tennis. Now it isn't just a mime.

On Learning The Form

In *The Tai Chi Club* first you learn what a move looks like by copying the movement. Then you learn one or two meanings which come relatively close to the actual way you are moving. As you wander down the Form the various ideas of using the 13 postures are explored, though usually not all at once as it is too confusing. It is the idea of controlling the energies of both yourself and an imagined opponent that are being explored, not individual techniques which you might have instigated. Also, most are performed with the idea of the other person being off balance, which you also have to achieve prior to doing anything. It can be broken down as follows:

1. What stance are you in and going into?
2. What are the arm (and later, kick, sweep) movements?
3. What is your body posture?
4. Where is your gaze travelling?
5. What is the meaning (Applications) of the movements?

On enjoying doing the Form.
How you do the Form internally is completely up to you, so while it's preferable to know the meanings of movement in one way or another it doesn't follow you have to think about them all, or even any of the time once you get the idea. The vast majority will have no interest or intention of ever having a fight or practising how to fight, but like to know if asked. They will just enjoy doing the movements, once they are known well, a sense of meditation can emerge which many find difficult to achieve by other methods such as trying to empty your mind. The moment you hear somebody tell you to sit still and empty your mind, you're probably dubious. You find many people can never stop thinking, life is too short. But in doing the mental challenge of trying to remember the moves you start to do them without thought and it's in those places you start to relax a little and eventually meditate and become more aware of your own self.

You are doing it wrong (Off message)
If the creator of Yang Tai Chi, Yang Lu Chan went to a modern Tai Chi session he would be told he was doing it wrong. His version would not match what was being taught, that's the deal you agree to at any

session. A teacher can't teach you what you know, only what they know. However, it's poor teaching to claim superiority of a style and state right and wrong, the exception being that you deliberately sought out a teacher known for their abrasiveness. In his youth Yang Lu Chan would have probably offered to test conclusions with such a teacher. It's reasonable to ask why you are doing something, but all of the Forms are made up and done by consensus. A person with a background on dealing with the elderly will know you are an idiot if you show moves they can't possibly perform. A person with a background in a hard martial style will have an idea of what works and what doesn't.

Just because a person teaches Tai Chi doesn't mean they know anything else of value. There is a story about a Tai Chi Master (it was put in to underline this very point, not to belittle his skill) who gave a lecture on the reason the Americans got to the moon first was because they were physically closer to it than the Chinese. Everybody brings their own experiences to the table, so while it's important to be open minded, don't ignore your instincts. If your little voice is telling you that you are being treated like an idiot, you probably are. If you find a genuine and athletic expert on Tai Chi Chuan, the initial thought will be you are in an ideal world. However, it will soon become apparent to the majority who find themselves in that position that they are never going to achieve the level being demonstrated because they can't put in the time required, or have the physical skill. That can be a very demoralising experience. Also those who are under thirty or studying hard styles and find themselves critical of some Tai Chi schools should consider this carefully. Are you sure you will keep it up for the rest of your life? If you aren't then tread carefully before you start judging others who are older and in your eyes, 'Not very good'. By the time you reach their age are you sure you will be still training?

On Instructors
You grab me here, then I'll stop you, so it must work. Anybody can look good if they write a script where they win. To show somebody applications, you do have to set the scene, the flaw in this presentation is real life isn't like that. If you are shown something and think with a little practise you could show it to other people or your knowledge has been added to regarding a movement, then great. But if you are just left with an overblown impression of the Instructor or start to believe leaving late and arriving first would be easy, then the demonstration

has missed its mark.
The aim of the Club is to help all those who come become better than the teachers provided they have that desire. Anybody can swallow books and then talk about levels, theory, say it doesn't translate, use Chinese terms to baffle and claim their teacher was the finest that ever walked the planet, but who really cares?

On Tai Chi Students
I talk sense all the time, you just listen intermittently. Most people don't really learn from the Instructors, within weeks almost everybody in the session is running at a different learning speed. It's not a race. The reality is most people do Tai Chi for one or two sessions, some for a couple of months, a few for a couple of years and a tiny minority of those who start, actually learn a full Traditional Form. By that time they will have forgotten more than they ever read or were taught. As for being worried what the Instructor thinks, forget it. The Instructors' main worry will be you won't show up. For the student the pleasure should come from the personal journey, learning from your friends and from your own pursuit of knowledge.

Review of The Ten Essential Principles

I've listed the ten from the head downwards in a basic format as it's easier to remember, but traditionally the sequence is Sink the Shoulders and Elbows listed after Solid and Empty Stance.

1. Straighten (lift up) the Head
Hold the head naturally erect. Not moving your head sideways or downwards. Lift up your spirits and try to be alert with your gaze. This encourages your Qi circulation and helps you to lead more Essence which in turn helps you raise up your Spirit further.

Qi, Spirit and Essence are the three things which help each other.

2. Sink the Shoulders and Elbows
You try not to raise up your shoulders, keep a slight space under your armpits and your elbows under control as these are easy to grab if care isn't taken. You want your lower body to be heavy and the upper body to be light. This is helped by imagining sinking down.

3. Correct Position of Chest and Back
Don't puff up the chest, let it relax down and stretch your back slightly by tucking in your tail bone.

4. Relaxation of Waist
Keep your waist around the lower 2nd vertebra loose and flexible.

5. Solid and Empty Stance
Clearly know which foot and where your majority of weight is being placed at any given point. As you shift the weight on your body from the left leg to the right, the leg taking the weight is towards full, the right towards empty and vice versa.

6. Co-ordination of Upper and Lower Parts
Everything moves as one, don't just move an arm or leg on it's own, it's a full body movement. Sinking your chest (3) helps your left and right side connect together. The energy comes from your feet (soles, Bubbling Well), explodes through your leg, is controlled by your waist and shown by your hands or feet.

7. Importance of Continuity
Everything moves as one so try to keep your movements and energies flowing. You make a circle from one move to the next.

8. Harmony between the internal and external parts
Know what the moves mean with regard to the 13 Postures. From the inside (internally) thinking about what your imagined partner is doing, and reacting (externally) to that situation. Then your internal energy can be co-ordinated together with your external movement.

9. Use the Mind Instead of Force
Keep relaxed so you can use speed and energy redirection rather than force.

10. Tranquillity (Stillness) in Movement
Stay calm and focused on what you are doing in the moment. Later this leads to the idea of 'Move late, arrive first' because you are calm and free to react.

A good method is to go through these in your mind (one at a time over a period of practise) as you stand in Preparation position adjusting your body to suit. Don't try and make your body fit a posture it doesn't like. Try to stand naturally with your legs neither locked nor bent. As you move through the Form have a go at maintaining one idea at a time, such as keeping the head upright, or keeping your shoulders relaxed downwards throughout each movement.

People new to the Form are probably best advised to just relax, stand naturally and breathe naturally.

Relax
As previously mentioned, by relaxing it doesn't mean become limp. You should feel energised inside and in control. It is a natural feeling. Try to feel your joints are open and extended. This is something that comes in time with familiarity of the moves and environment. Nobody is feeling particularly relaxed when learning something new in a new place. The idea is to be relaxed so your movements flow. Be easy on yourself. Give yourself time. Relax is the easiest thing to say and the hardest to put into action.

Stances

In the First Section there are effectively three stances, these are Parallel Stance, Bow Stance and Empty/Full Stance.

Parallel Stance (Horse stance)
This stance is done at its' most obvious in the Preparation, Beginning and End Postures as a relatively upright stance. However, you will save yourself a lot of time from a learning point of view if you notice that you are also going towards a parallel stance in terms of the position / angles of your feet on many occasions in the transition from Bow Stance to Bow Stance, Bow Stance to Empty Stance and Empty/Full Stance to Empty/Full Stance. But you are not standing up or bobbing up and down between the movements.

If you are moving from Left Bow Stance to Right Bow Stance, in the middle of the two you are positioning your feet towards a Parallel Stance and turning with waist movement from empty to full then back again.
Sometimes one foot will be slightly forwards when compared to the other, but the angle in comparison to the other foot will be towards parallel.

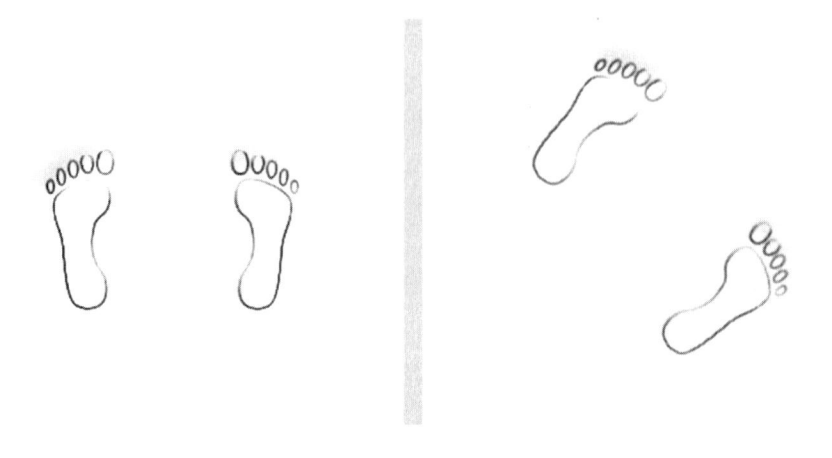

Bow Stance (Archer Stance)

This stance is done in an upright body posture such as 'Single Whip' and a leaning forward body posture such as 'Push'. The front foot in relation to your body you could imagine 90 degrees (or zero) pointing forwards and the back foot 45 degrees in relation to the front. The knee follows the toe in both legs so the back leg is not locked. The front knee should not go over the toe. You shouldn't feel like you could easily be pulled forward or pushed backward.

Feet are shoulder width (in loose clothing the back leg can appear to be straight) in general at the end of a posture the weight distribution is towards 60% on the front leg. The weight is also towards the balls of both feet.

(There is also a narrow off-diagonal or non-standard bow stance but this doesn't appear in the First Section). These guidelines are the aim, don't force your body into a position which feels uncomfortable or unstable.

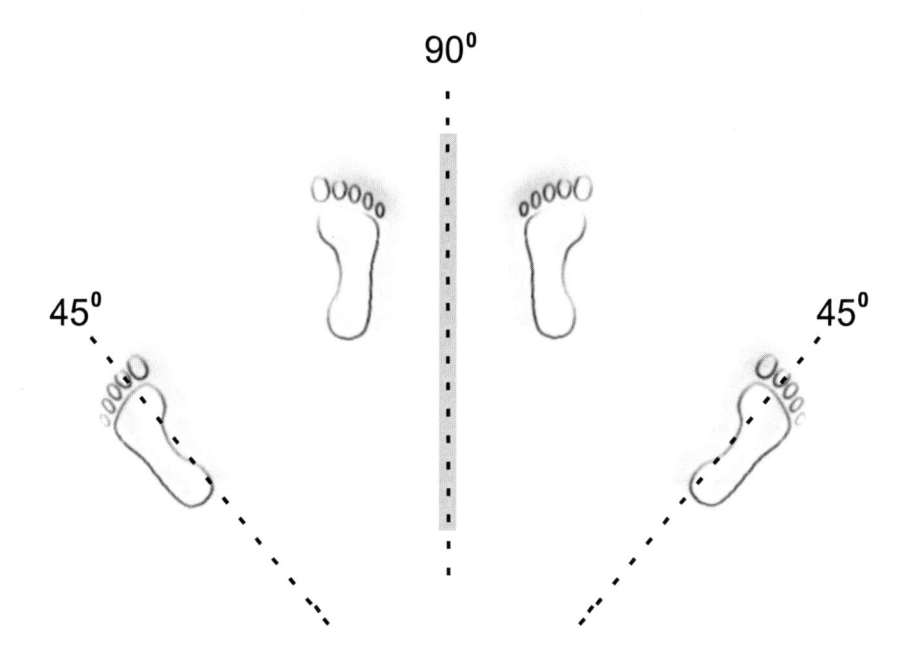

90^0

45^0 45^0

Bow Stance Leaning

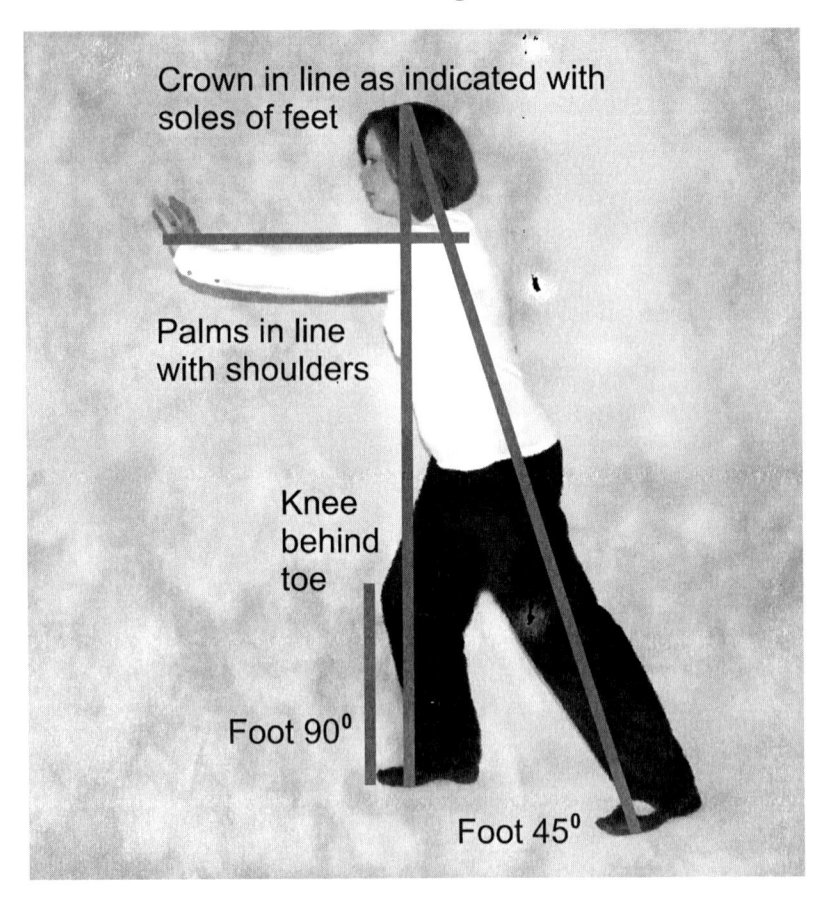

Crown in line as indicated with soles of feet

Palms in line with shoulders

Knee behind toe

Foot 90°

Foot 45°

Bow Stance Leaning Forward
Moving towards 'Push' posture.

Bow Stance
Upright

Bow Stance Upright
Moving towards 'Single Whip' posture.

Empty/Full Stance

This is done in an upright body position in two variations. The front foot in relation to your body could be imagined at 90 degrees (or zero) pointing forwards and the back foot 45 degrees in relation to the front. This stance is narrow compared to the bow stance with your front foot inner edge in line with the inner edge of your back heel. The weight is on the back leg as comfortably as you can manage (some use 70% as a guide). Knees follow the toes.

Variation 1. Front foot is on the ball. This can be thought of as being in a position to flick up a front leg kick with your weight on the rear. The front knee is towards bent (support).

Variation 2. Front foot is on the heel. This can be thought of as doing a sweeping technique to unbalance another persons step. The front leg/knee is towards straight (rooting) but not locked.

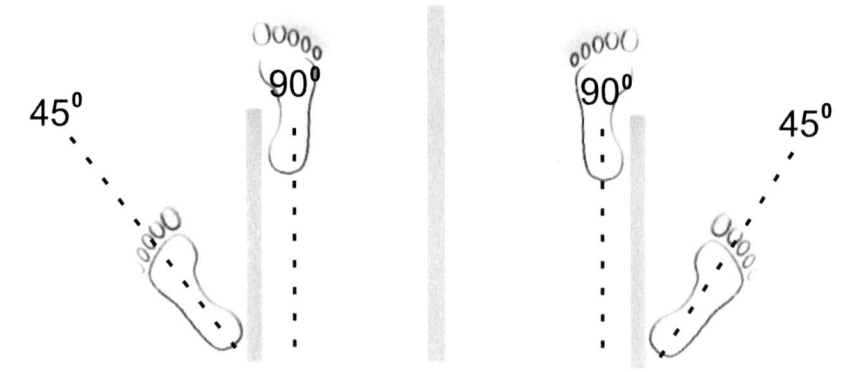

Transferring Weight
We generally begin and push with the rear leg and support with the front. The front leg can be used as a guide and brake to check you don't go forward too far or too little. The energy travels from one to the other. You don't allow the front leg knee to travel past the toe. You try to avoid bobbing up and down and should start off as you mean to go on, so don't go too low or step out too far. The movements should feel natural and you should feel you could change your mind (in theory at any point) and go back to your previous position if you wanted to.

Qi Gong & Form Introduction

Empty / Full
Stance 1

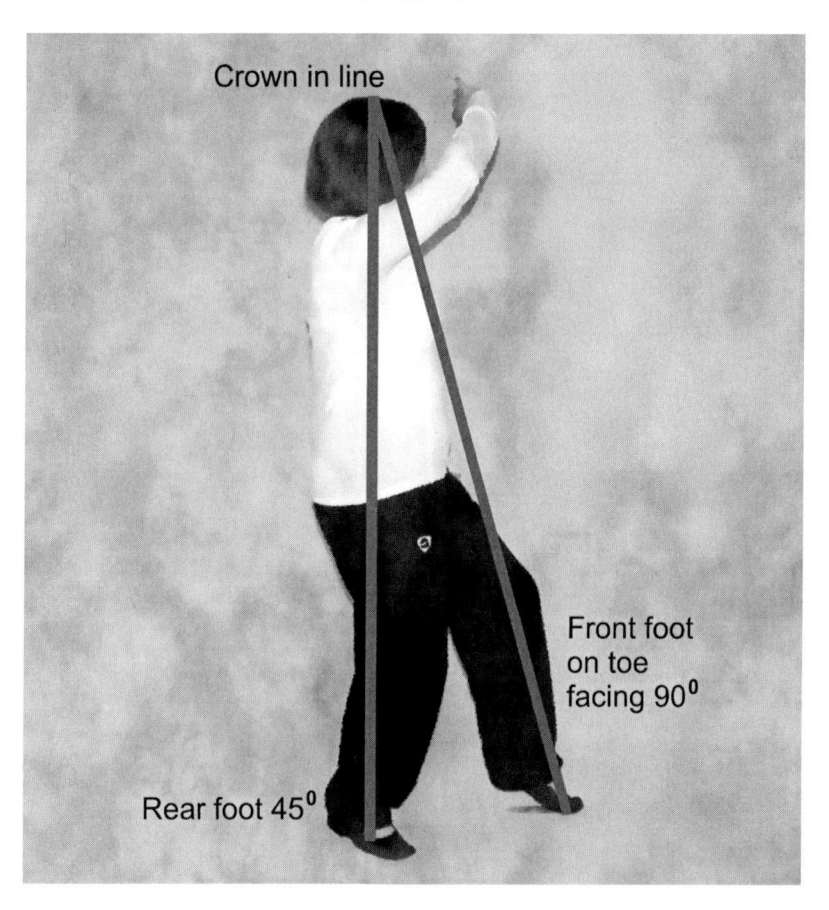

Crown in line

Front foot on toe facing 90⁰

Rear foot 45⁰

Empty/Full Stance On Toe
Moving towards 'White Crane' posture.

Qi Gong & Form Introduction

Empty / Full
Stance 2

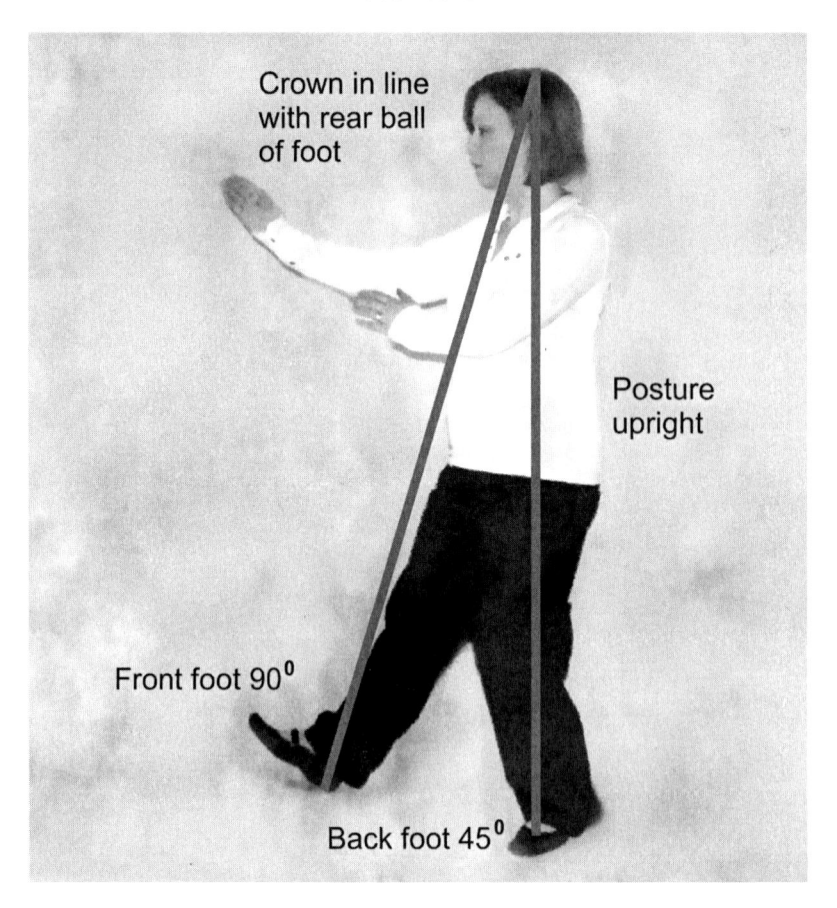

Crown in line with rear ball of foot

Posture upright

Front foot 90⁰

Back foot 45⁰

Empty/Full Stance On Heel
Moving towards 'Raise Hands' posture.

Hand Shape

There are three types which are **Palm**, **Fist** and **Hook**. Each one has various types of energy and intent which become more apparent when used with the idea of applications, but they look the same from an introductory point of view.

Further information

You make a Palm by extending the fingers slightly but not locked. Your fingers are slightly spaced and the thumb more open (Tiger Mouth). Not too tight or limp. Later all the uses of Palm are indicated with the same shape. To strike you turn your palm slightly to the side with your little finger towards your imagined partner. You do Push with your palms more towards facing the front (palms facing forwards towards a partner). The same palm shape is held in grabbing and so on.

You make a Fist by closing the finger gaps. Bend four fingers in with your thumb touching the top two fingers. The fist is a full fist, not empty (no peanut) but not too tight. The front of your fist is flat enough (like a boxer). The energy point varies, sometimes it is at the front, sometimes at the back, sometimes at the bottom of the fist or in the top two knuckles. There are also different ways the energy can be delivered. Sometimes you bend in (Fist Under Elbow) sometimes you go towards the straight (Parry, Block and Punch). Sometimes you chop outside (The Block in Parry, Block and Punch) or similar to Uraken Back Fist in Karate.

You make a Hook by turning your wrist down. The finger tips are close together with your thumb pressed to your middle and index finger. Don't make a small hook by bending in your fingers, which is more Chen style. The energy point is usually in the back of the palm (looks like Shoto-Uke) though it could be in the wrist or fingers depending on the intent. Remember everything is hidden. In applications a grab is a grab, a pull may require you to grip your opponent. This isn't shown, but is known to you, the practitioner. From a beginners perspective, other than changing between the three hand shapes, do nothing.

Direction: Your Back is to the North

When putting together instruction, direction is a really thorny issue. If you are with an Instructor then it's no problem because you can see which way they are moving in 3D in relation to the room. However, once you only have a book or video to view, everything changes because the cameraman has to decide does he take every shot from one angle, in which case many things will be obscured or does he take shots from different angles to make the moves clear, but then which way are they facing to follow the route of the Form? Anybody who has tried to learn a Form from film footage will know this problem very well.

The general consensus is to use the directions of a compass, not as simple as it sounds because many people don't really know which direction a compass is in relation to East and West and many styles use the compass differently. Yang Family following Yang Cheng Fu use it as your Back is to the North, which means you are facing South, with your right side facing West and your left side facing East. Unfortunately Yang Cheng Fu doesn't mention direction in his book *The Essence & Applications of Taijiquan* but Chen Weiming (who prefaced Cheng Man-ch'ing's Advanced Tai Chi Form Instruction book) does in *Taiji Sword And Other Writings* ("P.20) as does Yang Zhenduo in *Yang Style Taijiquan*.
(P.34.) "Hold body erect, facing forwards towards the South and looking straight ahead.".
I use these references because many people who practise various versions of Yang style both long and short do so facing the North. It's worth being clear which version is being used, as your back to the North means your right is West while if you are facing North it means your Right is East and you will turn the wrong way. As we practise the Form, these directions are based on the *Five Elements* and represented by the *Five Steps* on page 133.

So we do it starting in Preparation **Back to the North, facing South. Your right side is West, your left is East**. It's a good idea to practise and teach the moves in a room facing the same way, though it may not be practical to literally stand with your back to the magnetic North.

Qi Gong & Form Introduction

Direction

You face this way if a compass was on the floor.

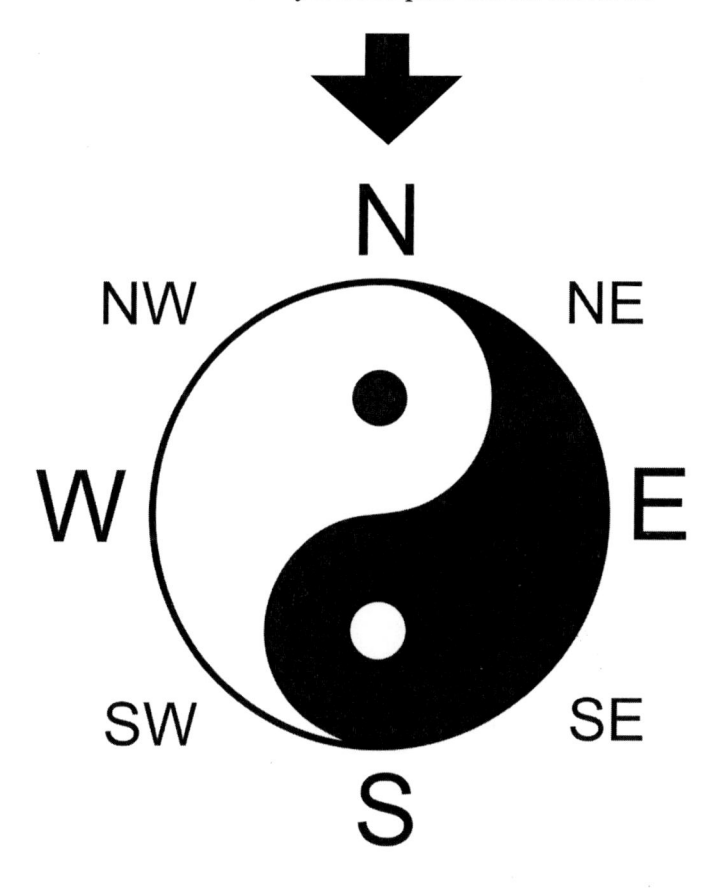

⬇

```
           N
    NW         NE


  W               E


    SW         SE
           S
```

East **Left** Wood **Green**
South **Forward** Fire **Red**
West **Right** Metal **White**
North **Back** Water **Black***Colourless
Centre **Centre*** Earth **Yellow**
(*Centre Equilibrium)

133

Chinese terms
I've tried to avoid using Chinese terms as much as possible because I think it is a real barrier to the newcomer who is interested, but despairs at the constant use of phrases which mean nothing to them. Phrases that I have used are **Qi** (Pronounced "Chee" as in "Cheese") and which can be thought of as Energy and **Dantien**, the middle point of the body.

Then of course there is **Tai Chi Chuan** or **Taijiquan** the literal translation often being cited as "Supreme Ultimate Fist" through using the idea of Yin and Yang to develop a fighting system. Chuan can also mean control both over self and a situation, so it could be stretched to a definition of "Supreme Ultimate System of Self-Control".

Nowadays, because of the Net and the efforts of many enthusiasts, information is widely available. Ten years ago if you wanted to know what a Form really looked like, you had to send off for DVD's from Taiwan (and often it wasn't very much like the versions being taught in the UK). Today if film exists you can see it on You Tube. That opening up of information has caught a lot of the old guard out. You can't bluff it so easily. All the founders of Tai Chi are long dead and while the secrets can be passed on, the physical skill cannot, everybody has to learn it for themselves from move one.

Conclusion
Tai Chi is a doing thing, so if you are put off by all the books and Chinese 'ology, that you haven't got a Chinese Master on your doorstep or feel you are not very good, relax.

Just do your best with what you've got and enjoy doing it. That is perhaps its' most important message.

Neil Bradley
06/06/2011

Session Structure

Open sessions with a Wushu Greeting

Make a fist with the right hand, put it against the centre of the left palm with the left thumb bent and the four other fingers of the left hand stretched, push the two hands forward with the palms facing those greeted, arms in an embracing position and shoulders dropped down.

Meaning
The aim is to show we come together with integrity and modesty, our fist covered and extending friendship.

Remember to keep within your comfort zone.

Optional Warm Up (Meridian Tapping is also treated as a warm up.)

Head to Toe Routine:

> Neck rotations (clockwise & anti clockwise)
> Shoulder rolls (clockwise & anti clockwise)
> Arms extended out to the side, rotate wrists (clockwise & anti clockwise)
> Shake hands (side, front arms out, front arms bent)
> Waist turning left and right, arms slapping front & back of body (hips straight)
> Hip rotations (clockwise / anti-clockwise)
> Knee bending (forwards and back, don't rotate)
> Right / Left leg picked up (Out, In and Knee down)
> Left / Right ankle rotations (clockwise & anti clockwise)
> Left & Right outside edge foot rolls on floor
> Left and right leg. Stretching of extended leg and gentle opening of ball & socket in bent leg

Keep your back straight throughout, point the toe of your bent leg out 45 degrees towards the corner, both knees in the direction of toes.

Meridian Double Hand / Finger Tapping

10, 13 and/or 18 Postures

Form
We run through the form as a group and demonstrate each movement as the group progresses. Encourage each other to teach and understand the movements by example.

Three Circles
Draw three circles from up to down / Out to in. On the in circle, palms keep above the elbows then push down.

Meaning
The setting of the Sun/Moon a relaxation of learning and a time for rest, the end of the session.

Close

Review of Movement Names
1st Section

1. Preparation Form
2. Beginning *(Commencing Form)*
3. Grasp the Birds' Tail *(Sparrows')*
4. Single Whip
5. Raise Hands and Step Forward
6. White Crane Spreads *(Displays)* its Wings
7. Left Brush Knee and Push *(..and Twist Step)*
8. Hand Strums the Lute *(Pipa, Guitar)*
9. Left Brush Knee and Push
10. Right Brush Knee and Push
11. Left Brush Knee and Push
12. Hand Strums the Lute
13. Left Brush Knee and Push
14. Step forward, *(Deflect Downward)* Parry Block and Punch
15. Apparent Close Up
16. Cross Hands

In brackets are other common versions used to describe similar movements.

Recommended Reading.

Yang Chengfu The Essence & Applications of Taijiquan Translated by Louis Swaim
Yang Style Taijiquan by Yang Zhenduo
Fu Zhongwen Mastering Yang Style Taijiquan Translated by Louis Swaim
—
The Dao Of Taijiquan by Jou, Tsung Hwa
Steal My Art T. T. Liang by Stuart Alve Olson

LAO-TZU: "My words are very easy to understand." CMC Lectures Translated by Tam C. Gibbs
The Tao Teh Ching Translated by James Legge
The Tao of Pooh by Benjamin Hoff

The Root Of Chinese Qigong by Dr Yang, Jwing-Ming

Chen Style Taijiquan by Feng Zhiqiang & Feng Dabiao
Taiji Sword and Other Writings by Chen Weiming
Tai Chi Chuan Decoding The Classics by Dan Docherty

Resources

The Tai Chi Union For Great Britain
www.taichiunion.com

International Yang Family Tai Chi Chuan Association
www.yangfamilytaichi.com

Tai Chi Finder - Locate Instructors by Region - Online store
www.taichifinder.co.uk

The Tai Chi Club
www.TheTaiChiClub.co.uk

Notes

Qi Gong & Form Introduction